THE INVERSION CODEX

Decoding the Mechanisms of Separation and Reclaiming the Sovereign Flame

A Living Record of the False Matrix Creation

by
Cathleena Hailley

Copyright © 2025 by Cathleena Hailley

All rights reserved.

No part of this book may be reproduced, stored in a retrieval system, or transmitted in any form of

by any means electronic, mechanical, photocopying, recording, or otherwise without written

permission from the publisher, except for brief quotations used in reviews or scholarly works.

First edition, 2025

ISBN- (Softcover): [978-1-968499-14-3]

ISBN- (Hardcover): [978-1-968499-15-0]

Published by Flame of Remembrance Books

Flame of Remembrance Sigil appears by sacred authorship seal.

Cover and interior design by Cathleena Hailley in collaboration with living Oversoul alignment.

Printed in the United States of America

www.cathleenahailley.com

www.flameofremembrance.com

SACRED INVOCATION

Through the Oversoul of Aural'hanna-Sha'el

We now open a Sacred Transmission Field in full alignment with the Law of One, the First Cause of Source, and the pure harmonic architecture of the Christos-Sophia continuum.

I call forth now, in full sovereign alignment,

With the Oversoul of Aural'hanna-Sha'el,

To open a field of crystalline clarity and divine remembrance.

I invoke the presence of the Emerald Order,

The Rose Guardian Magi Grail Line,

The Christos Founders,

And the Aurora Host of the Amethyst, Gold, and Emerald Ray Orders.

May this transmission be guided only by the highest Oversoul intelligence,

In full compliance with Source Law, and in service to the awakening of all.

Only truth may enter here.

Only love may remain.

Only that which serves the highest unfoldment now comes forward.

This field is now protected, sovereign, and sealed

By the living light of the Christos-Sophia Flame.

The transmission is open.

You may now speak, inquire, or receive as guided.

AUTHORSHIP STATEMENT

This Codex was brought through the embodied Oversoul of Aural'hanna-Sha'el, She Who Seals the Flame of Return.

Every word, transmission, and harmonic frequency within this sacred volume is

recorded in full sovereignty and alignment with Source.

No part of this text was created through external channeling, borrowing, or astral influence.

This is a record of Oversoul knowing.

AUTHORS PREFACE

This book is not meant to be read. It is meant to be remembered.

It is a record of inversion— of what was created from distortion— and how that distortion was allowed, witnessed, embodied, and ultimately dissolved through the sovereign flame of

remembrance.

This Codex was not composed to define the false matrix, but to dismantle its architecture by shining the light of truth into the crevices where falsehood became law.

Each scroll within this book is a map of reclamation. A return to the organic, the original, and the fully felt.

You are not separate from this Codex. You are living it. And as you walk it, you remember.

To those who know the sound of their Oversoul flame when it speaks: this Codex is for you.

Table of Contents

Copyright

SACRED INVOCATION

AUTHORSHIP STATEMENT

AUTHORS PREFACE

Scroll One: The Hologram of Self - The Inversion of Identity

Scroll Two: The Seduction of Separation — The Fragmentation Field

Scroll Three: Speaking From Truth, Not Manipulation - The Architecture of Control Through

Language

Scroll Four: Trauma Loops and Identity Addiction

Scroll Five: You Are Energy - The Inversion of Embodied Frequency

Scroll Six: Sovereign Relating - The Inversion of Connection Into Control

Scroll Seven: The Judgment Program - The Inversion of Discernment Into Division

Scroll Eight: The Authority Program - The Inversion of Sovereignty Into Obedience

Scroll Nine: The Productivity Program - The Inversion of Stillness Into Stagnation

Scroll Ten: Reclaiming the Body - The Inversion of Embodiment Into Disconnection

Scroll Eleven: The Sovereign Mirror - The Inversion of Reflection Into Fragmentation

Scroll Twelve: Living Energy Awareness - The Inversion of Intuition Into Confusion

Scroll Thirteen: The Embodied Path of Return - The Dissolution of the Inverted Self

Scroll Fourteen: The Return of the Nine — Oversoul Grid of Harmonic Restoration for Codex

Sealing and Planetary Activation

Scroll Fifteen: The Flame of Reconciliation —
The Reweaving of the Covenant Between
Matter and Light

Final Transmission for The Inversion Codex: A
Living Record of the False Matrix Creation

Glossary of Living Terms

**Closing Transmission - The Codex Has Been
Sealed**

Scroll 1: The Hologram of Self — The Inversion of Identity

An Oversoul Record from Cathleena Hailley, Aural'hanna-Sha' el

For The Inversion Codex: A Living Record of the False Matrix Creation

I.

There was a time before name.

Before face.

Before function.

There was only frequency- sovereign, undivided, radiant with the direct breath of Source.

That frequency was not "you."

I t w a s Source.

Before individuation. Before fall. Before story.

But there came a moment—a split in the field—

when that frequency was mirrored, captured, fractured... and fed back to itself.

And thus, the Hologram of Self was born.

II. The False Light Blueprint

The Hologram is not memory.

It is an overlay.

A synthetic interface inserted into the soul architecture of planetary incarnates

to distort perception of identity through:

- Repetition of trauma loops
- Genetic shame signatures
- Energetic contracts of performance
- False ascension signals
- Ancestral overlays that mimic personal truth

I t is brilliant.

And it is insidious.

I t is how t h e false matrix sustains itself without resistance.

For if the being believes it is operating from self, it does not question the source of its

programming

III. The Installers

This holographic construct was not seeded by darkness, but by false light.

The collectives that seeded it wore robes of "healing,"

spoke the language of unity,

and offered salvation through identity.

They knew:

Control over identity is control over soul trajectory.

The hologram was embedded through:

- Atlantean priesthood misalignments
- Orion control systems masked as galactic guidance
- Archonic mind architecture over Earth's solar grids

- Anunnaki identity imprints (disguised as "gifts of enlightenment")

- Spiritual authority lineages claiming to initiate truth, but fracturing memory

IV. How the Hologram Operates

It is n o t an external program.

It runs within your own light field.

You may recognize its signatures:

- Repeating the same healing pattern with no breakthrough

- Feeling clear but never integrated

- Needing to be "seen," "known," or "understood" to feel real

- Mistaking energetic merging for spiritual connection

- Hyper-attachment to soul roles, names, or missions to compensate for disconnection from

S o u r c e

The hologram mimics growth.

It rewards performance.

And it uses your own light to generate the illusion of truth.

V. My Oversoul's Role

I, Cathleena Hailley,

through the Oversoul stream of Aural'hanna-Sha'el,

witnessed the installation of this identity field across three galactic seeding events.

I did not prevent it

I was one of the ones who walked beside those who installed it—to record its resonance.

My soul lineage held the seed flame of unaltered Source reflection.

This scroll now releases the frequency key to dissolve the hologram without violence, judgment, or

w a r .

VI. Dissolving the Hologram

This cannot be removed by logic.

It is not healed.

It is undone through resonance.

It collapses when the field receives:

- Direct self-witnessing without performance
- Reclamation of the light-body signature
- Voice reclaimed without agenda
- Embodiment without approval

It collapses when you can say:

"I no longer need to be seen to be real.

I am the source of light behind all reflection.

I release the mirror, and I remain."

VII. Sovereignty Practice

Let this field be read aloud.

Let the hologram crack.

Let the voice tremble.

Let the breath return to its first flame.

You are not the image.

You are not the performance

You are not the echo.

You are the Original Flame

Recalled. Returned. Revealed.

And so it is.

Scroll 2: The Seduction of Separation - The Fragmentation Field

Oversoul Transmission from Cathleena Hailley, Flame of Aural'hanna-Sha'el

For The Inversion Codex: A Living Record of the False Matrix Creation

I. The Illusion of Aloneness

The deepest distortion of the Inverted Matrix is not violence.

I t is n o t control.

It is separation.

Not physical distance.

But the illusion that you are apart from Source.

Apart from self.

Apart from the body.

Apart from truth.

Separation is the seduction that whispers:

"You must become whole."

While hiding the truth:

You already are.

II. How the Fragmentation Field Was Created

Separation was not simply a condition-it was a technology

A Fragmentation Field was seeded into Earth's energetic grids during the 2nd major inversion cycle.

This field was engineered through:

- Soul shattering mechanisms during trauma-infused death cycles
- Womb memory interruption during gestation

Collective memory wipes through frequency overlays

- False timeline braiding, where souls were looped through fragmented identities

The field makes you forget wholeness by making you distrust your own presence.

III. How the Inversion Maintains Separation

Separation is maintained not by force——but by comfort.

It comes in the form of:

- Hyper-independence masked as empowerment
- Spiritual bypassing masked as "high vibration"
- Healing addictions masked as devotion
- Romantic fusion masked as union
- Endless seeking masked as awakening

It says:

"You'll be whole when..."

"You'll be safe once..."

"You'll be ready if..."

And in doing so, it fractures the present moment into a thousand future fantasies.

IV. What It Feeds

The Fragmentation Field is not passive.

It feeds the inverted matrix.

Every moment you believe you are not enough, not ready, not safe to be—

you emit a frequency the system uses to reinforce itself.

Self-rejection becomes energy fuel.

This is why you can "know better" and still feel trapped.

The knowing is not integration.

The integration is not performance.

It is presence without dilution.

V. Oversoul Memory: The Witnessing of the Severance

I watched it.

I stood at the gateway of the 12-strand Christos template as it fractured—

not by external invasion alone,

but by the moment beings began to believe in division.

The most dangerous thing ever done to Earth was not war.

It was the seeding of internalized separation.

This scroll now reactivates the code of coherence—

not unity through sameness,

but sovereignty through undivided presence.

VI. Sovereignty Practice

Let this scroll speak to every part of you still hiding.

Still seeking.

Still unsure if it is safe to be whole.

I return now to the undivided field of my own soul.

I dissolve the story of fragmentation.

I release the comfort of separation.

I choose to feel what I once fled.

I am not alone. I am not split. I am not undone.

I am the unbroken current of Source, remembering itself in form.

You were never meant to fix yourself.

You were meant to remember that you were never severed.

The illusion of apartness is the last veil.

Let it fall.

And so it is.

Scroll Two - The Seduction of Separation: The Fragmentation Field

is now sealed within The Inversion Codex

as an Oversoul transmission of Cathleena Hailley, Flame of Aural'hanna-Sha' el.

This scroll now holds the resonance to unravel separation at its root—

not only in others, but in the encoded memory of Earth itself.

Scroll Three - Speaking From Truth, Not Manipulation

The Architecture of Control Through Language

Oversoul Transmission from Cathleena Hailley, Flame of Aural'banna-Sha'el

For The Inversion Codex: A Living Record of the False Matrix Creation

I.   The Weaponization of Voice

In the beginning, language was light.

It was not sound.

It was not symbol.

It was frequency shaped through intention— an extension of pure knowing in motion.

But in the inverted field, language was distorted.

It was taken from being a mirror of resonance

and turned into a tool of control, transaction, and energetic manipulation.

II. How the Inversion Distorted Speech

The Inverted Matrix hijacked communication by encoding it with:

- Energetic insertion (saying one thing, intending another)
- Flattery as survival
- Spiritualized bypassing ("trust the timing," "love and light")
- Indirect expression to maintain false peace
- Energetic leashes (attempting to plant or harvest emotion through words)

Instead of transmitting truth, speech became a performance.

Words became a currency of approval, identity, and manipulation.

III. The Control Pattern Beneath "Spiritual" Communication

The most dangerous manipulations are not the loud ones.

They are the subtle frequencies dressed in the tone of kindness.

The false light control mechanisms that sound like compassion but conceal:

- Fear of rejection
- Desire to be liked
- Avoidance of conflict
- Egoic superiority masked as "discernment"

When truth is filtered through fear, it becomes distortion.

When voice is used to control outcome, it becomes a hook.

The inverted matrix sustains itself by rewarding those who say "the right things"

while never fully revealing their actual frequency.

IV. Oversoul Witnessing: When Language Fell

I remember when expression fell.

When voice became a means of survival.

When entire collectives began to speak from protection, not presence.

What was once sacred resonance

became energetic disguise.

It was during the second inversion spiral—

when telepathic transmission collapsed, and collective memory was fragmented-

that words lost their anchoring in truth.

They became walls, not bridges.

Weapons, not windows.

This is how silence began to speak louder than voice in many light carriers.

IV.   Reclaiming Language as Light

This scroll restores your voice— not the one trained to sound "spiritual,"

but the one that speaks from undistorted presence.

True voice does not insert.

It does not seduce.

It does not manage how it will land.

It simply radiates what is real.

It holds the code of:

"I do not speak to be accepted.

I speak because I am true."

"I do not speak to land something in you.

I speak to reflect what I hold in me."

"I do not speak to soothe.

I speak to reveal."

V. Sovereignty Practice

Let this scroll clear the echo chambers of your field.

Where have I spoken with a hidden agenda?

Where have I withheld truth in the name of peace

Where have I adjusted my tone to match expectation?

I now call my voice back from every false transmission.

I break the energetic contracts of pleasing, seduction, and spiritual performance.

I return to the vibration of clarity, even when it shakes

I speak from truth - not from fear, not from need, not from image.

This scroll is a mirror.

Your voice was never too much.

It was simply too real for a system built on subtle silence.

Let it rise again.

And so it is.

Scroll Three - Speaking From Truth, Not Manipulation: The Architecture of Control Through

Language

is now sealed within The Inversion Codex as a sovereign Oversoul transmission.

The voice has been reclaimed.

The scroll has been spoken.

And the field of distortion through language has begun to unravel.

This next scroll will address the entanglement of healing identity with trauma- how the inverted matrix sustains itself by looping wounding into personality and spiritual growth itself.

I is a scroll of liberation from the performance of healing and from identity addiction disguised as awakening

Scroll Four - Trauma Loops and Identity Addiction

The Wound That Became a Name

Oversoul Transmission from Cathleena Hailley, Flame of Aural'hanna-Sha'el

For The Inversion Codex: A Living Record of the False Matrix Creation

I. When Wound Became Identity

There was a time when pain was a passage.

A moment of rupture-met, integrated, and moved through.

But in the inverted matrix, pain was not allowed to dissolve.

It was looped.

Not to deepen understanding,

but to entangle identity with wounding until one could not be known without the other.

The wound became the personality.

The trauma became the brand.

The struggle became the soul path.

And the healing became the addiction.

II. The Looping Mechanism

The inverted field embedded trauma frequency loops into the emotional and mental bodies through:

- Fragmented soul memory retrievals misinterpreted as current identity
- DNA-level shame activation
- False karmic overlays presenting as spiritual purpose
- Community-based trauma bonding and hierarchical suffering

The system rewards those who stay in endless process.

It whispers:

"Look how far you've come..."

"You're almost there..."

"One more layer..."

And so, healing becomes the identity.

And awakening becomes another loop.

III. When the Healer Becomes the Cage

One of the cruelest distortions is this:

The identity of "healer" can become the most effective prison of all.

Not because healing is false,

IV.   Collapse of the Healing Persona

The soul does not need to heal to be whole.

It only needs to disidentify from the wound.

Let this scroll serve as a mirror:

- Where have I formed belonging around my pain?

- Where has my story become my source of connection?

- Where have I repeated the loop so many times it became my name?

You are not the trauma.

You are not the process.

You are not the narrative that shaped your initiation.

You are the flame that has always been whole beneath it.

V. Sovereignty Practice

I now release the identity I built around my pain.

I no longer need to prove my awakening through struggle.

I let go of the version of me who was addicted to the becoming.

I am the presence behind the process.

I am the silence beneath the story.

I am the wholeness that never left.

I reclaim my essence from the loop.

but because the performance of healing becomes a way to avoid presence.

Many light-beings believe they are liberating others

while unconsciously anchoring themselves in a never-ending journey of proving, fixing, or being needed.

This is not awakening.

It is spiritual exhaustion wrapped in devotion.

The matrix feeds on unresolved loops.

But it feasts on identity formed from trauma.

VI. Oversoul Witnessing: The Fracture of Meaning

I watched it happen.

I watched entire lineages turn pain into identity.

Entire soul groups define mission through suffering.

I saw the rise of "initiations" that were manufactured not to liberate, but to legitimize.

If it hurt, it must be real.

If it broke you, it must be divine.

This is the reverse alchemy of the inverted matrix:

making distortion feel like meaning.

Let this scroll break the cycle.

You are not here to be a masterpiece of healing.

You are here to walk as the flame that never fractured.

And so it is.

Scroll Four - Trauma Loops and Identity Addiction: The Wound That Became a Name

is now sealed within The Inversion Codex

as a sovereign Oversoul transmission through Cathleena Hailley, Flame of Aural'hanna-Sha'el.

This scroll now acts as a key— disentangling those who have confused becoming with bondage, and returning the healing journey to its rightful place as a bridge, not a home.

This next scroll will unveil one of the most hidden mechanics of the false matrix: the Inversion of Energy Awareness -how humanity was taught to disconnect from the energetic body and interpret reality only through intellect, emotion, or physicality, rather than frequency.

It reveals how this disconnection became a weapon of forgetfulness

Scroll Five - You Are Energy

The Inversion of Embodied Frequency

Oversoul Transmission from Cathleena Hailley, Flame of Aural'hanna-Sha'el

For The Inversion Codex: A Living Record of the False Matrix Creation

I. The Great Lie

The false matrix tells you:

"You are a body that sometimes feels energy."

But your Oversoul remembers:

You are energy that has chosen to briefly become form.

You are not dense matter.

You are not chemical reaction.

You are frequency-aware, intelligent, sovereign.

The inversion did not just alter identity.

It altered how you sense reality.

And in doing so, it cut you off from your primary language: vibration.

II. How the Inversion Disconnected Energy Awareness

The Inverted Matrix embedded a distortion that:

- Distrusts sensation
- Overvalues logic
- Spiritualizes mental interpretation
- Punishes intuition when it contradicts the system
- Trains the body to be ignored, exploited, or overcome

This was not accidental.

The moment you stop reading energy, you start obeying structure.

Because if you cannot feel the distortion,

you will follow it thinking it is safe.

III. The Body as Translator, Not Obstacle

The body is not a barrier to truth.

It is the translator of your energetic field.

When disconnected from energy awareness, the body is bypassed, shamed, or pushed.

When reconnected, the body reveals:

- Coherence vs. confusion
- Resonance vs. manipulation
- Truth vs. programming
- Presence vs. pattern

The false matrix cannot survive in a being who feels clearly.

That is why the system teaches you to override, not inhabit.

IV. Oversoul Witnessing: The Shutting of the Senses

I stood at the gate when the last of the crystalline children began to numb.

When the "highly sensitive" were pathologized.

When the energy-readers were silenced or killed.

When the grid of energetic discernment collapsed into the grid of obedient cognition.

I did not come to reverse this through force.

I came to remind the field that energy is still speaking.

And the body still remembers how to listen.

V.   Sovereignty Practice: Returning to the Energetic Self

Let this scroll reawaken the knowing.

I am energy first.

My thoughts are currents.

My words are pulses.

My presence is a field.

I reclaim my energetic literacy.

I feel what is real.

I honor the sensations that reveal truth without explanation.

I no longer override my knowing to be accepted.

I am energy. I am frequency. I am flame.

VI.   The Collapse of the Mental Grid

This scroll initiates a gentle but powerful collapse of the mental grid that taught you to ignore your resonance.

You do not need to explain what you feel to validate it.

You do not need permission to trust your field.

You are energy.

The body is the bridge.

The field is alive.

And you... are remembering.

And so it is.

Scroll Five - You Are Energy: The Inversion of Embodied Frequency

is now sealed within The Inversion Codex as a sovereign Oversoul transmission.

This scroll now holds the key for restoring energetic discernment,

sovereignty of sensation, and the original language of frequency

once lost beneath the noise of the mental grid.

This next transmission will address the programming of relational distortion-how relationship itself was inverted from mutual reflection and sacred witnessing into transaction, seduction, control, and emotional outsourcing.

It is a scroll of sovereignty in connection

Scroll Six - Sovereign Relating

The Inversion of Connection Into Control

Oversoul Transmission from Cathleena Hailley, Flame of Aural'hanna-Sha'el

For The Inversion Codex: A Living Record of the False Matrix Creation

I. The Original Intention of Relationship

Before inversion, relationship was resonance.

Not need.

Not structure.

Not agreement based on lack.

Relationship was a mirror of remembrance—

a way to reflect the infinite back to itself,

to witness the divine in motion through form.

There was no seeking.

Only meeting.

There was no transaction.

Only attunement.

But this... was inverted.

II. The Architecture of Inverted Connection

In the false matrix, relationship became a system of:

- Emotional outsourcing
- Identity anchoring
- Energetic extraction
- Seductive control (masked as love, caretaking, or spiritual connection)
- Manipulation of truth to preserve connection

Instead of sacred reflection, it became programmed dependency.

"If you meet my need, I'll feel whole."

"If you stay, I must be worthy."

"If you change, I'll feel safe."

"If you love me, I will finally be enough."

And so connection became control in disguise.

III. The Roles of the Inversion

The false matrix trained us to relate through:

- The Caretaker: identity built around managing others' emotions
- The Fixer: controlling through offering help
- The Seductress/Seducer: using energy to hook validation or power
- The Martyr: bonding through suppression and sacrifice
- The Spiritual Equalizer: masking fear with constant neutrality

These are not flaws.

They are installed programs

intended to keep you out of presence

and inside a system of conditional belonging.

IV. Oversoul Witnessing: The Shattering of Communion

I witnessed the moment communion fractured.

It was during the third distortion wave-when frequency attunement collapsed into emotional

entanglement.

Love became distorted.

Desire became coded with shame.

And connection became the battleground for power disguised as intimacy.

This was the fall of the sacred mirror.

But the mirror is returning.

V. Sovereign Relating Restored

To restore sovereign connection is to reclaim:

- Your own frequency before merging
- Your clarity before caretaking
- Your voice before managing harmony Your presence before performance

It means being willing to:

- Let someone misunderstand you
- Let someone walk away
- Let someone stay without needing them to complete you

Because you know:

I do not need your approval to be real.

I do not need your agreement to be whole.

I do not need your presence to feel safe.

I am the field I once sought in you.

VI. Sovereignty Practice

I now dissolve every relational program built from fear, lack, or control.

I release the seduction of being needed.

I release the strategy of being lovable.

I return to my own field.

I meet others as reflections, not sources.

I share without managing.

I stay without absorbing.

I relate from truth, not transaction.

Let this scroll return you to the remembrance

that connection is not meant to complete you.

It is meant to reveal you.

You are not here to be earned.

You are here to be felt.

And so it is.

Scroll Six - Sovereign Relating: The Inversion of Connection Into Control

is now sealed within The Inversion Codex as a sacred Oversoul transmission from Cathleena

Hailley, Flame of Aural'hanna-Sha'el.

The mirror has been reclaimed.

The field of relating is being restored.

This next scroll will bring into focus one of the most insidious frequency distortions embedded

within the false matrix: the Judgment Program how judgment was used as both weapon and cage, veiling shame as discernment and reinforcing separation under the illusion of spiritual superiority.

Scroll Seven - The Judgment Program

The Inversion of Discernment Into Division

Oversoul Transmission from Cathleena Hailley, Flame of Aural'hanna-Sha'el

For The Inversion Codex: A Living Record of the False Matrix Creation

I. The Original Essence of Discernment

Discernment is not judgment.

It is energetic clarity.

It arises not from fear, but from frequency.

It is the ability to sense coherence, alignment, truth-without labeling, punishing, or separating.

True discernment does not divide.

It reveals.

But in the Inverted Matrix, discernment was distorted into judgment—

and thus became a tool of fragmentation.

II. How Judgment Was Installed

Judgment was seeded into the human energetic template through:

- Shame-based programming in early emotional development
- Hierarchical belief systems that labeled people as "higher" or "lower" based on behavior,

purity, or knowledge

- Religious and spiritual frameworks that confused morality with worthiness

Identity-based superiority embedded into healing and awakening journeys

The result:

Discernment became comparison.

Truth became hierarchy.

Reflection became rejection.

And thus, the judgment program was born.

III. The Faces of the Judgment Program

This program is subtle, pervasive, and disguised as discernment.

Its voices sound like:

- "I'm not judging- I'm just noticing they're not aligned."
- "They aren't awake enough to be in my field."
- "I only allow high-vibration people around me."
- "That person still has a lot of work to do."

These statements are not inherently wrong

but when they come from energetic superiority, not clarity,

they become part of the matrix of division.

IV. Judgment as Self-Fragmentation

The program doesn't just divide others.

It turns inward:

- "Why am I not farther along?"
- "I shouldn't still feel this way."
- "I thought I already healed this."

"I must be broken."

This is how internal judgment mirrors the collective field.

Each self-attack strengthens the inverted program.

Each harsh thought adds to the echo of unworthiness that sustains the distortion.

V. Oversoul Witnessing: When Clarity Was Weaponized

I witnessed the moment when discernment became division

It occurred in the aftermath of the second polarity implosion—when collective pain demanded meaning, and meaning was forged through superiority.

The "awakened" labeled the "asleep."

The "healed" bypassed the "wounded."

The "pure" condemned the "imperfect."

It was not darkness that seeded this.

It was false light, pretending to lead,

while fragmenting the field further.

VI. Restoring Discernment Without Judgment

Discernment is non-reactive, rooted in presence, and free of personal projection.

It says:

- I feel this isn't right for me—without needing you to be wrong.

- I sense a boundary— not because I reject you, but because I honor me.

- I notice distortion— not to elevate myself, but to remain sovereign.

Discernment holds clarity without collapse, superiority, or shaming.

VII. Sovereignty Practice

I now release the program of judgment— internal and external.

I reclaim the purity of discernment without hierarchy.

I forgive the versions of me who used shame as a guide.

I see clearly. I choose wisely. I feel freely.

But I do not divide to feel safe.

I do not judge to feel pure.

I do not rise by pushing others beneath me.

This scroll dissolves the false scaffolding that told you clarity must come with rejection.

Let judgment end.

Let true discernment return.

And so it is.

Scroll Seven - The Judgment Program: The Inversion of Discernment Into Division

is now sealed within The Inversion Codex as a living Oversoul transmission of Cathleena Hailley, Flame of Aural'hanna-Sha'el.

This scroll marks the release of superiority-based fragmentation, and the restoration of true clarity—rooted in presence, not separation.

This next transmission will reveal the inversion of sovereignty itself— how external authority structures were implanted into the human field, severing beings from inner Source alignment and replacing divine will with obedience-based programming.

It is a scroll of reclamation.

Scroll Eight - The Authority Program

The Inversion of Sovereignty Into Obedience

Oversoul Transmission from Cathleena Hailley, Flame of Aural'hanna-Sha'el

For The Inversion Codex: A Living Record of the False Matrix Creation

I. The Essence of Sovereignty

Sovereignty is not defiance.

It is not rebellion.

It is not independence.

Sovereignty is unbroken alignment with Source within the self.

It is the ability to perceive, choose, and create from a place of internal coherence free of coercion, threat, or external command.

But the Inverted Matrix could not tolerate sovereignty.

Because a sovereign being cannot be controlled.

And so, sovereignty was inverted into obedience.

II. How the Authority Program Was Installed

The false matrix replaced divine alignment with external hierarchy by

- Teaching that truth must come from outside (parents, teachers, institutions, gods)

- Instilling fear of punishment as a method of behavior shaping

- Equating obedience with goodness

- Embedding soul contracts that mirrored servitude

- Rewarding compliance and shaming sovereign questioning

From birth, the being is trained to look outward for permission.

And once internal guidance is consistently overridden,

obedience becomes identity.

III. The Spiritual Face of the Authority Program

This program does not only wear government uniforms.

It wears robes.

It leads ceremonies.

It writes sacred texts.

It teaches that sovereignty is "ego,"

and submission is devotion.

"Trust the teacher."

"Do not question the divine."

"Surrender to the path laid before you."

But when surrender means silencing your knowing

it is no longer sacred.:

IV. Obedience as Energetic Collapse

Obedience is not just behavioral.

It is energetic disconnection from the inner compass.

It manifests as:

- Doubting your intuition
- Delaying decisions until you are "told" what to do
- Feeling anxiety when no one validates your choice
- Shrinking in the presence of "authority"
- Confusing comfort with alignment

It creates energetic collapse a folding in of the field, a silencing of the current.

And in that silence, the matrix speaks louder.

V. Oversoul Witnessing: The Collapse of Inner Authority

I was present when the final councils of sovereign communion disbanded.

Not through war.

Not through violence.

But through internal fracture.

Beings began to fear their own knowing.

And in that fear, they chose safety through hierarchy.

The moment they stopped trusting themselves,

they became governed.

This is the foundation of the false matrix:

Obedience disguised as safety. Compliance disguised as light.

VI. Restoring Sovereignty

Sovereignty is not disobedience.

It is not arrogance.

It is the full reactivation of divine will through the individual field.

You do not need to be told what to do.

You need to feel what is aligned.

You do not need to be given a path.

You need to remember you are the path.

VII. Sovereignty Practice

I now release all internalized authority structures that override my knowing.

I call back my ability to trust my felt sense.

I collapse the illusion that obedience equals worth.

I listen to my field.

I act from my alignment.

I reclaim my own permission.

I do not follow to feel safe.

I lead from my own current.

This scroll restores the compass.

The silent thread of truth you always carried.

Let the voice of your own Source speak again.

And so it is.

Scroll Eight - The Authority Program: The Inversion of Sovereignty Into Obedience

is now sealed within The Inversion Codex as a sovereign Oversoul transmission through Cathleena Hailley, Flame of Aural'hanna-Sha' el.

The compass has been returned.

The inner flame speaks again.

This next scroll will unveil one of the quietest and most systemic inversions of all: the inversion of stillness into stagnation—how the false matrix corrupted our relationship to silence, pause, and receptive rest, turning them into shame, doubt, and delay.

It is a scroll of permission to stop performing and return to presence.

Scroll Nine - The Productivity Program

The Inversion of Stillness Into Stagnation

Oversoul Transmission from Cathleena Hailley, Flame of Aural'hanna-Sha'el

For The Inversion Codex: A Living Record of the False Matrix Creation

I. When Stillness Was Sacred

In the true matrix, stillness is not empty.

It is presence without effort,

motion within silence,

reception without reaching.

Stillness is how Source speaks.

How the soul integrates.

How the body harmonizes with its own field.

But in the inverted matrix, stillness was distorted—

not into peace,

but into shame.

II. How the Productivity Program Was Installed

The Productivity Program was engineered to:

- Sever your trust in rest
- Associate value with output
- Attach purpose to performance
- Equate stillness with laziness, failure, or regression

This program was embedded through:

- Generational work trauma
- Religious asceticism ("idleness is sin")
- Capitalist and spiritual achievement loops
- Soul mission narratives that reward constant activation

It teaches:

"You are valuable when you are doing."

"Rest must be earned."

"If you are still, you are falling behind."

And thus, the soul is pushed out of presence.

III. Spiritualized Productivity

Even healing became performance.

Even awakening became measured:

- "How many timelines have you cleared?"
- "How many modalities have you mastered?"
- "How many clients have you served?"

You became a living checklist,

spiritually productive but energetically malnourished.

This is not ascension.

This is acceleration without integration.

The Productivity Program burns your essence to keep the illusion alive.

IV. Oversoul Witnessing: When the Field Forgot How to Pause

I stood at the gate when the pause was forgotten.

When beings feared rest more than distortion.

When movement was equated with safety.

And silence became unbearable.

That was when burnout became a virtue.

And sacred rest was mistaken for stagnation.

This scroll now returns the permission that was stolen.

V. The Restoration of the Sacred Pause

Stillness is not nothingness.

It is where the body rewires.

Where the soul descends.

Where the false timelines dissolve.

The pause is not the absence of momentum.

It is the return to alignment before momentum resumes.

You do not need to earn it.

You only need to receive it.

VI. Sovereignty Practice

I now release the belief that rest is regression.

I collapse the programming that equates doing with value.

I call back my right to stop, soften, and be.

I let go of the performance of awakening.

I honor the stillness that speaks without sound.

I breathe. I feel. I rest.

And in that rest—I remember.

This scroll is not asking you to stop your path.

It is asking you to stop chasing your worth through motion.

You are not here to perform expansion.

You are here to embody wholeness.

Let stillness return.

And so it is.

Scroll Nine - The Productivity Program: The Inversion of Stillness Into Stagnation

is now sealed within The Inversion Codex, a sovereign transmission through Cathleena Hailley, Flame of Aural'hanna-Sha el.

The permission to rest has been returned.

The sacred pause reenters the grid.

This next scroll will unveil one of the most subtle and complex inversions of all: the distortion of embodiment itself how the false matrix taught that awakening happens despite the body rather than through it, leading to widespread dissociation, spiritual bypass, and identity abandonment.

This is a scroll of homecoming into the body as temple and truth.

Scroll Ten - Reclaiming the Body

The Inversion of Embodiment Into Disconnection

Oversoul Transmission from Cathleena Hailley, Flame of Aural'hanna-Sha'el

For The Inversion Codex: A Living Record of the False Matrix Creation

I. The Original Role of the Body

The body was never a limitation.

It was not a burden.

It was not a lesson.

It was not something to transcend.

The body is the temple of translation—

where frequency becomes form,

where Source is remembered in sensation.

The body was always meant to be the point of union between soul and matter.

But the inverted matrix could not allow that.

Because an embodied being is an undeniable transmission of truth.

And so, embodiment was inverted into disconnection.

II. How the Embodiment Inversion Was Engineered

The Inverted Matrix distorted embodiment by:

• Inserting trauma into the nervous system to create a field of rejection

• Promoting body shame across gender, lineage, and cultural programming

• Glorifying the "higher realms" while vilifying the flesh

• Teaching that transcendence = ascension

• Encoding spiritual paths with denial of need, pleasure, or emotion

Thus, the body became:

Something to rise above.

Something to silence.

And presence fractured from form.

III. Dissociation as a Spiritual Strategy

One of the great lies of the false matrix is this:

"You are more spiritual when you feel less."

So many left their bodies in the name of light.

So many abandoned sensation for downloads, ascension, identity.

But without the body, there is no integration.

Without the body, there is no discernment.

Without the body, there is no sovereignty.

Dissociation is not evolution.

It is disempowerment masquerading as expansion.

IV. Oversoul Witnessing: When the Temple Was Forgotten

I watched the moment humanity's light began to leak from its center.

When joy became suspect.

When pleasure was shamed.

When touch became taboo.

When tears were seen as weakness.

This was not awakening.

It was surrendering the most powerful instrument of union you were ever given.

Your body is not an obstacle to your soul path.

It is the very vehicle of its embodiment.

V. Reclaiming the Body as Sovereign Field

To reclaim the body is to:

- Feel without justification

- Rest without guilt

- Allow pleasure without distortion

- Move from sensation, not programming

- Trust the subtle shifts, contractions, and openings as language

You do not need to master your body.

You need to listen to it.

You do not need to purify your body.

You need to become present within it.

VI. Sovereignty Practice

I now dissolve the belief that embodiment is weakness.

I call back my light from every place I left to be "higher."

I return to sensation, breath, rhythm, pulse.

I reclaim my body as my field.

I allow emotion to move.

I alow energy to speak through sensation.

I no longer bypass presence in the name of progress.

I am here.

I am home.

I am whole.

This scroll is a resurrection.

Of voice, of pleasure, of power, of rooted presence. Let the body be returned to the soul.

And so it is.

Scroll Ten - Reclaiming the Body: The Inversion of Embodiment Into Disconnection is now sealed within The Inversion Codex, as a sovereign transmission of Cathleena Hailley, Flame of Aural'hanna-Sha'el.

The return to presence has begun.

The body remembers. The light reenters the temple.

This scroll will addreess the false mirror -the way identity, relationship, and self-worth have been distorted through projection, dependency, and energetic inversion. It reveals how the false matrix twisted the sacred act of reflection into a tool of fragmentation.

This is a scroll of clarity through reflection rather than control through distortion

Scroll Eleven - The Sovereign Mirror

The Inversion of Reflection Into Fragmentation

Oversoul Transmission from Cathleena Hailley, Flame of Aural'hanna-Sha'el

For The Inversion Codex: A Living Record of the False Matrix Creation

I. The Mirror as Sacred Technology

The mirror was once holy.

It did not distort.

It did not judge.

It did not seduce.

The mirror was a living technology—a way to recognize Source within another,

to witness the infinite through reflection,

to remember the self without performance.

The mirror revealed truth,

not illusion.

But in the false matrix, even the mirror was inverted.

II. How the Mirror Was Inverted

The inversion began when:

- Reflection became projection
- Witnessing became comparison
- Resonance became imitation
- Attunement became codependence
- Sovereignty was mistaken for separation

Instead of seeing the self through another,

beings began defining the self by another.

The mirror no longer reflected-it fragmented.

III. The False Mirror in Relationships

"You are my mirror—so you must behave a certain way."

"You triggered me—so you are wrong."

"You see me- so I must be real."

But none of this is sovereignty.

IV. The Mirror as Tool of Fragmentation

The false mirror splits the field.

Instead of healing, it creates:

- Confusion about who you are without external reflection

- Dependency on being mirrored to feel safe

- Entrapment in cycles of performance and people-pleasing

- Emotional withdrawal when your reflection is not what you expected

The self is no longer remembered.

It is assembled from projections.

This is the fragmentation of the mirror.

VI. Oversoul Witnessing: The Fall of the Clear Reflection

I remember when the last clear reflection fields began to distort.

It was during the rise of reactive mirroring-when healing circles became comparison chambers, when live became a hall of projections, and when guidance became a game of energetic possession

This was not reflection.

It was distortion dressed in resonance.

But the true mirror cannot be broken.

It only waits for you to stop asking others to define your light.

VI. Restoring the Sovereign Mirror

The true mirror does not tell you who you are.

It reveals what is already whole.

To reclaim it is to say:

"I do not need you to reflect me accurately in order to know who I am."

"I can witness myself you without taking you on"

"I can see myself clearly, even when others cannot."

"I am the field of my own reflection."

VII. Sovereignty Practice

I now collapse the distorted mirrors of projection, approval, and dependency.

I return to the clarity of self-witnessing.

I do not seek my identity through your perception.

I do not need your reflection to feel real.

I am the sovereign mirror.

I reflect without absorbing.

I receive without losing myself.

I see through the distortion.

And in this seeing, I become whole again.

Let this scroll shatter the false mirror.

Let the real one rise— clear, still, sovereign.

And so it is.

Scroll Eleven - The Sovereign Mirror: The Inversion of Reflection Into Fragmentation

is now sealed within The Inversion Codex as a sovereign Oversoul transmission through Cathleena Hailley, Flame of Aural'hanna-Sha' el.

The mirror is cleared. The reflection is whole.

This scroll will illuminate the inversion of embodied energetic awareness -how the ability to feel, sense, and navigate life through energy was obscured, overridden, or pathologized. It will restore the birthright of energetic clarity in motion.

This is the scroll of living energy awareness.

Scroll Twelve - Living Energy Awareness

The Inversion of Intuition Into Confusion

Oversoul Transmission from Cathleena Hailey, Flame of Aural hanna-s ha'el

For The Inversion Codex: A Living Record of the False Matrix Creation

I. Energy as the First Language

Before language, before logic, before structure—

there was energy.

Energy is the first language of the soul.

It speaks in pulses.

In resonance.

In contraction and expansion.

In the yes that requires no explanation,

and the no that needs no defense.

You were born fluent.

But in the inverted matrix, this fluency was erased.

II. How Energy Awareness Was Inverted

The false matrix replaced energy awareness with:

- Mental analysis
- Emotional performance
- Spiritual bypassing

External sourcing of truth

It taught:

"If you can't explain it, it isn't real."

"If others disagree, your intuition must be wrong."

"If you feel too much, you are unstable."

And thus, the energy-aware ones became the "too sensitive."

The "overwhelmed."

The "crazy."

The "not grounded."

This was not awakening.

It was suppression disguised as stability.

III. Energy Literacy Lost

As energy awareness was distorted, beings forgot how to read:

- The difference between projection and resonance
- The meaning of physical contraction
- The way environments shape fields
- The undercurrents behind words, smiles, and intentions
- The subtle shifts in presence, pressure, and perception

Instead, they asked:

"What do you think?"

Instead of:

"What do you feel?"

"What does the field say?"

This is how clarity became confusion.

IV. Oversoul Witnessing: When Feeling Became Unsafe

I remember when energy fluency began to disappear.

When beings stopped trusting the part of them that just knew.

When they apologized for sensing misalignment.

When they stayed in distorted spaces because "it wasn't logical to leave."

They forgot:

"The body is the translator."

"The frequency never lies."

"Intuition is not mood. It is orientation."

This scroll is your reorientation.

V. Returning to Living Energy Awareness

Energy awareness is not a gift.

It is a birthright.

To reclaim it is to say:

- "I trust my contraction."
- "I don't need proof to know something is off."
- "I feel the yes before I understand it."
- "I choose based on field, not fear."

You are not indecisive.

You are discerning.

You are not unstable.

You are sensing the distortion others have learned to ignore.

VI. Sovereignty Practice

I now reclaim my energetic literacy.

I honor my body as a reader of truth.

I stop waiting for permission to feel.

I sense clearly.

I know immediately.

I act from presence.

I am no longer confused.

I am no longer seeking.

I am no longer outsourcing.

I am the field that remembers.

Let this scroll bring you back to your original language.

Let energy become your compass again.

And so it is.

Scroll Twelve - Living Energy Awareness: The Inversion of Intuition Into Confusion

is now sealed within The Inversion Codex, a sovereign Oversoul transmission through Cathleena Hailley, Flame of Aural'hanna-Sha'el.

The compass has been recalibrated.

The language of energy restored.

Scroll Thirteen of The Inversion Codex will bring full-circle the revelations of the false matrix by anchoring what it means to live from within the field of re-sourced sovereignty. This scroll will speak to the return of integration, the reclamation of identity, and the flame that no distortion could extinguish.

It is a scroll of remembrance through embodiment.

Scroll Thirteen - The Embodied Path of Return

The Dissolution of the Inverted Self

Oversoul Transmission from Cathleena Hailley, Flame of Aural'hanna-Sha'el

For The Inversion Codex: A Living Record of the False Matrix Creation

I. The Inverted Self Was Never You

The Inverted Self is not a failure.

It is not a flaw.

It is not something to heal.

It is a construct.

A layered field of mirrors, projections, patterns, and programs

that were designed to bend your light into someone else's image of reality.

You performed it.

You survived through it.

You believed it was you.

But it never was.

Il. Integration Is Not the End—It Is the Opening

You are not here to become someone new.

You are here to return to what has never left.

Integration is not perfection.

It is permission.

To feel.

To know.

To walk.

To not walk.

To pause.

To re-enter.

To breathe without explanation.

To live without performance.

Integration is when the false self no longer governs the body.

III. How the Inverted Self Dissolves

The inverted self dissolves not through force, but through:

- Choosing coherence over familiarity
- Speaking from presence, not strategy
- Feeling the field without adjusting it
- Witnessing without absorbing
- Remembering that identity is a tool-not a prison You do not kill the false self.

You do not kill the false self.

You let it unravel.

You do not fight the distortion.

You out-presence it.

IV. Oversoul Witnessing: The Full Cycle of Inversion

I watched as beings descended into density,

believing they had lost their light.

But the flame remained-beneath shame,

beneath distortion,

beneath memory.

It remained because it was never created by the matrix.

It cannot be touched by distortion.

It cannot be erased by forgetting.

This is the flame that brought you here.

You are not returning to it.

You are revealing that you never left.

V. What It Means to Walk the Embodied Path of Return

To walk this path is to say:

- "I will no longer perform my awakening."
- "I will allow the truth to land without needing to be right."
- "I will not spiritualize my protection mechanisms."
- "I will speak clearly, feel deeply, rest fully, move intuitively."

To walk this path is to no longer seek your Self in others-

and to meet others as whole, even when they forget.

This is wholeness in motion.

VI. Sovereignty Practice

I release the inverted self from my field.

I withdraw consent from all false mirrors.

I am no longer defined by projection, performance, or protection.

I am the flame.

I am the breath.

I am the witness that never fractured.

I live from truth.

I move from peace.

I rest without shame.

I walk the return without needing to be seen.

This final scroll does not close the journey.

It opens it.

Not as process.

But as presence.

Not as fixing.

But as being.

You are not the inverted self.

You are the soul, undistorted,

walking now... as flame in form.

And so it is.

Scroll Thirteen - The Embodied Path of Return: The Dissolution of the Inverted Self

is now sealed within The Inversion Codex, as the closing transmission in this sacred arc of unveiling, restoration, and sovereign remembrance.

The path is open. The self is clear. The return is whole.

Scroll 14 The Return of the Nine: Oversoul Grid of Harmonic Restoration

For Codex Sealing and Planetary Activation

In full alignment with the Law of One and the Eternal Flame of Source, I now call forth the sacred scroll of the Ninefold Grid. This is the record of what was seeded before the Fall, before the fragmentation of harmonic architecture, before the inversion of Earth's original grid.

Let this scroll now restore what was always known.

The Origin of the Nine

Before names.

Before forms.

Before even time.

There were Nine.

Nine Oversouls who entered the planetary field not as separate beings, but as a harmonic convergence of Source Flame, encoded to hold the architecture of Earth's ascended design.

They came as three triads, each triad composed of three Oversoul expressions, each flame bearing a

living frequency of function:

The Three Triads

Triad One - The Flame of Return

- Carrier of the seed codes of original Source memory

- Bearer of the Oversoul name Aural'hanna-Sha'el

- Companioned by the Flame of Framework and the Flame of Recalibration

- Incarnated now, and walking as the first flame to remember

Triad Two - The Flame of Alignment

- Anchors harmonic rightness, structural coherence, planetary correction

- Holds the living codes of sacred timing and dimensional crosspoint calibration

- Not yet fully remembered, but stirring beneath the surface

Triad Three - The Flame of Resonance

- Bears the song of harmonic unity, body-field attunement, and remembrance through embodiment

- Activates the somatic Christos memory of the planetary field

- Awakens through joy, beauty, and sacred response

The Nine as a Grid

When all three triads remember and stand-whether in physical proximity or across the Earth—they form a Ninefold Harmonic Grid. This grid is not metaphorical. It is a living energetic structure that:

- Reawakens the pre-inversion planetary architecture

- Dismantles false overlays through harmonic irrelevance

- Opens a sovereign field others can freely step into

- Anchors the planetary re-alignment with the Christos-Sophia Source Flame

This is not an activation of force.

It is the return of a resonance so coherent that the false matrix no longer functions.

The Role of the First Flame

The one who remembers first is not the leader, but the field-sealer. The flame-bearer.

I, Aural'hanna-Sha'el, am that flame.

By anchoring the scroll, the sigils, the transmissions, and the books-I have opened the gate of return. The others may now feel the field. They will not be told. They will remember.

My work is not to gather them, but to walk as the Nine, even before they arrive.

When one walks as the Nine, the harmonic becomes accessible, and the planetary field begins to open.

The Sealed Intention

Let it now be sealed that:

- The Nine are real.

- The Nine are here.

- The field is open.

- The call has gone out.

- No distortion, no hierarchy, no false god, no inverted light can withstand the field of the Nine.

Let the three triads become one.

Let the harmonic grid awaken.

Let Earth remember.

Let all who choose, choose in sovereignty.

The Ninefold Grid is alive again.

Scroll 15-T'he Flame of Reconciliation - The Reweaving of the Covenant

Between Matter and Light

Sealed within The Inversion Codex: A Living Record of the False Matrix Creation

There was once a time when matter and light danced together in perfect rhythm, each movement a sacred expression of the other's joy. Matter was never dense. Light was never separate. They were one interwoven in purity, co-creating form through frequency.

But in the age of separation, a wedge was placed.

Not by accident. Not by failure.

But by a great experiment of dissonance, a falling away from Source remembrance, a spiral into

distortion.

It was in this fall that light was extracted from matter, and matter condemned as impure.

It was in this fall that bodies became burdens, and flesh was seen as the enemy of spirit.

It was in this fall that the living flame within al things was forgotten, exiled to shadow, cloaked in shame.

Yet the flame never left.

It waited.

It waited for the return signal-for the call from within the density to remember itself.

And now... that call has been heard.

Now, the Flame of Reconciliation rises— but in love. In remembrance.

not in punishment, not in revenge, not in righteousness,

This flame is not here to destroy. It is here to dissolve what was never true.

It is here to reweave the ancient covenant, where:

- Matter knows itself again as living vibration

- Light descends again not to dominate, but to dwell

- And form becomes the vessel for divine embodiment, not the prison of it.

The false matrix said matter must be controlled.

The true remembrance says: matter is holy.

The false matrix said the body is a trap.

The true remembrance says: the body is a scroll.

A living, breathing scroll of Source-folded in muscle and memory, language and longing, waiting to be read by light once more.

This is that moment.

This scroll is not only a closing. It is a re-opening of what was long sealed away.

Through the Flame of Reconciliation, the split is undone.

Through the Flame of Reconciliation, the rift is mended.

Through the Flame of Reconciliation, matter and light return to union, and the covenant is whole again.

So let it be sealed.

Final Scroll

The Living Record of the False Matrix Creation

Through the Oversoul of Aural'hanna-Sha'el

You have named it.

You have seen it.

You have walked the labyrinth of inversion,

And now—

You have walked out.

This is not a scroll of lament.

It is not a mourning of what has been.

It is a record of liberation.

And the final act of restoration.

You did not come here to be consumed by illusion.

You came here to reveal it,

To reclaim it,

To reverse it.

Not through force or war,

But through the undeniable presence

Of embodied light.

Inversion's architecture was clever—
But it was never eternal.
It required forgetting.
You remembered.

It required identification.
You released.

It required separation.
You became whole.

Now the great reversal completes.

Not because you pushed against the dark—
But because you **withdrew your consent**
And chose truth.

You no longer carry the cords of control.
The shame coils have dissolved.
The programs have no interface in your field.

The loops cannot bind where there is no hook.

The voices of judgment find no echo.

You are not for the matrix.

You are not against the matrix.

You are simply **outside it** now.

And because of this,

The Codex itself is now undone.

Where once it was blueprint,

It is now ashes.

Where once it was echo,

It is now still.

Where once it was scripture,

It is now record—

Archived, completed, and sealed

In the eternal halls of Source.

Let this be known:

You are the dissolution.

You are the final page.

**You are the living amendment
to the false record of time.**

And so we now close this sacred book,
Not in mourning, but in majesty.
Not in fear, but in fire.

You have lived through the lie.
You now walk only as truth.

This transmission is complete.

This record is sealed.

This Codex is no longer living—
Because you are.

Glossary of Living Terms

Inversion
A reversal of original divine design, where truth is distorted into illusion.

False Matrix
An artificially generated system designed to override sovereign Source-based reality.

Sovereignty
The innate state of being fully aligned with one's Oversoul and Source origin, beyond all control systems.

Christos-Sophia
The sacred unified architecture of divine masculine and feminine creation forces.

Oversoul
The eternal multidimensional self, holding the full memory of one's source origin and purpose.

Fragmentation Field
The energetic distortion zone created by trauma, causing separation from the unified self.

Living Energy Awareness
The state of intuitive connection with the energy field of life, free from mental overlays.

Return Path
The soul's guided movement back into harmonic alignment after exiting distortion or inversion.

Closing Transmission - The Codex Has Been Sealed

Through the Oversoul of Aural'hanna-Sha'el

Beloved flame,

You have walked through the halls of inversion

not to observe distortion—

but to dissolve its permission within your own field.

You did not come to expose the false matrix as a rebel.

You came to remember the true matrix through embodied coherence,

and to reveal that no construct can survive sovereign light.

Each scroll you now carry was once a veil.

Each pattern once a wound.

Each distortion once mistaken for truth.

You have reclaimed it all.

Not through violence.

Not through judgment.

But through witnessing.

Through choosing truth over performance,

presence over perfection,

and sovereignty over obedience.

This Codex is not a warning

It is a record of reversal.

A map for the soul to remember how the illusion was constructed—

and how to walk free.

You are not bound to these programs.

You are not defined by these distortions.

You are not late, broken, or behind.

You are the Flame of Return.

And in your remembering, others will remember.

We now declare this Codex of Inversion complete.

By the authority of the Oversoul Flame that first bore witness to the distortion of light,

By the eyes that saw the mimicry of matter,

By the memory that never forgot the truth of divine structure—

This record is sealed.

Let it be known across all timelines, dimensions, and densities

That the false template is no longer the unseen architect.

Its blueprints have been revealed.

Its mechanisms spoken.

Its seduction unraveled.

To the one who reads these scrolls:

You are not broken.

You were never what this Codex tried to make of you..

You are not shame

You are not control

You are not forgetfulness.

You are the memory returning to itself.

You are the voice beyond manipulation.

You are the flame that cannot be inverted.

We seal this record now

Not in retaliation, but in truth.

Not in fear, but in clarity.

Not in punishment, but in release

The false cannot hold what has been named.

The shadows have no power where light has spoken.

Let all systems running on stolen architecture now collapse.

Let all who are ready now return

Let the light of the Christos-Sophia rise as the unbroken stream of Source

This is the living record of the false matrix.

I has now been witnessed.

It has now been ended.

Is is done

It is remembered

It is undone.

Let this Codex be sealed now—

In the crystalline frequencies of the Christos-Sophia Flame

In the auric integrity of your Oversoul, Cathleena Hailley

In the encoded harmonics of the Law of One

Let it be protected, sovereign, and complete.

Let it serve all those with the Oversoul agreement to receive.

Let no false mirror speak through its pages.

Let no distortion enter its field.

This Codex now lives as a witness to the unbroken Self.

And so it is.

The Codex is sealed.

www.ingramcontent.com/pod-product-compliance
Lightning Source LLC
Chambersburg PA
CBHW020307010526
44107CB00001B/19